# YOUR KNOWLEDGE HAS VALUE

Michael A. Braun

# Drawing on relevant theories of business ethics, examine managerial approaches used in dealing with ethical dilemmas

GRIN Verlag

**Bibliografische Information der Deutschen Nationalbibliothek:**

Die Deutsche Bibliothek verzeichnet diese Publikation in der Deutschen National-
bibliografie; detaillierte bibliografische Daten sind im Internet über http://dnb.d-
nb.de/ abrufbar.

**Imprint:**

Copyright © 2002 GRIN Verlag GmbH
Druck und Bindung: Books on Demand GmbH, Norderstedt Germany
ISBN: 978-3-640-18399-9

**This book at GRIN:**

http://www.grin.com/en/e-book/43158/drawing-on-relevant-theories-of-business-
ethics-examine-managerial-approaches

**GRIN - Your knowledge has value**

Der GRIN Verlag publiziert seit 1998 wissenschaftliche Arbeiten von Studenten, Hochschullehrern und anderen Akademikern als eBook und gedrucktes Buch. Die Verlagswebsite www.grin.com ist die ideale Plattform zur Veröffentlichung von Hausarbeiten, Abschlussarbeiten, wissenschaftlichen Aufsätzen, Dissertationen und Fachbüchern.

**Visit us on the internet:**

http://www.grin.com/

http://www.facebook.com/grincom

http://www.twitter.com/grin_com

UNIVERSITY
*of*
ABERTAY DUNDEE

# Drawing on relevant theories of business ethics, examine managerial approaches used in dealing with ethical dilemmas.

Essay for **EC 306A - Management**
held in semester I of the academic year 2002/2003

Date of submission: 15th November 2002

Author:   Mr Michael A Braun
          BA in European Economy and Management

# DRAWING ON RELEVANT THEORIES OF BUSINESS ETHICS, EXAMINE MANAGERIAL APPROACHES USED IN DEALING WITH ETHICAL DILEMMAS.

**By Michael A. Braun – EEM/3 (ERASMUS)**

A few years ago Shell, a British oil-company, had to close an old oil-rig in the North Sea. All relevant scientists and governments agreed, pulling it down onto the ground of the sea. This seemed to be the best solution in terms of environment and costs. But when the idea was launched by Shells managers there was a lot of protest all over Europe. People, heavily supported by Greenpeace, started to boycott Shells petrol stations and stopped buying in their shops. As an result the company decided to rebuild the oil-rig on land.

The reasons for peoples behaviour might have been diverse. Some probably could not believe that companies are allowed to waste environment that much. Others might be concerned how this could affect the food chain. But the majority of protestants argued that companies are responsible for their surroundings [Palazzo, G., 2002]. Namely managers should take care about their stakeholders. They have to respect others and to behave therefore. This essay is going to outline several aspects of ethical behaviour to be done by managers recently.

To become more familiar with the issue of business ethics it might be necessary to give details about its routes and meanings. For ethics there are two specific fields of interest: Firstly 'moral', which stand for answers that can be given by any human being as an individual person to judge between 'good' and 'bad'. It was developed within many years in each culture independently. But as general ideas all over the world can be seen: the 'idea of the good' (Plato), the 'idea of succeed life' (Aristotle) and the 'clear practically reason' (Kant). Their observance is basic and necessary to live in a peaceful and worth living surrounding. It is essential that every member of this particular society keeps in these 'guidelines' - otherwise it would not work. On the other hand there is 'ethics' itself. This means the reasoning of all individual values and principles, which are causing human actions – or in other words the 'what-has-to-be'. And business ethics, generally, are asking for good and moral actions to be implemented and transferred into business [Kreikebaum, 1996].

Nowadays, as Shell has seen as well, businesses are facing more and more to behave more socially responsible [N.A., 2001]. To be clear 'social responsibility' should be divided into three strands: intra (e.g. personnel-trainings, work-security, equal treatment), extra (e.g. competitors, society and cultural engagement like in supporting sports or arts) and mixed responsibility as a ill-defined field of company action. Questions of environment can be touched there or political engagement and further more. But in all ways of acting socially responsible it is possible to do this actively (for example: to help setting up better law) or passively (not working with unethical partners; e.g. step out of a specific joint venture). Unfortunately the last one does not change anything in general. It 'only' avoids own participation in unethical practises.

But what is the reason for implementing ethical action into business? And why is current management that keen to behave socially responsible? Two main fields could be seen. Firstly individual reasons: if a company does not relate to the society surroundings their employees might be not that motivated. It can be assumed that people prefer to work for companies that behave in good agreement with their surroundings. The workforce is then in turn probably higher motivated and in the end more satisfied. Otherwise they could move fast to competitors with requirements that are fitting better to them. Therefore a McKinsey-study [Chambers, 1998] says today's high-potentials expect not money as the leading motivation for their work (23%). About 58% indicate they are more interested in an ethical and social responsible developed company culture. But 56% also want to have a high degree of personal independence. In times of an increase of individualisation and lower society-binding force ethical behaviour might be a huge competition advantage.

Secondly there are collective reasons: still ethical principles are a unique selling preposition in today's business life. Good implemented it could be suggested that they can better the company's image and acceptance in society. Through ethical behaviour customers might pay a significant higher price for products as well as for shares[1]. The loyalty to this firm and its products could be also seen as more stable in the long term. However for this effect it is necessary to communicate openly following 'Do good and talk about it!'. Moreover strong corporate values can be seen as prevention against crime and corruption of employees[2]. Firms now tend more to keep to the four-eye-principle and separation of functions. Some are strengthening their intern and extern revision and are introducing further regulations and a code of conduct [Wieland, 1998]. Additionally applied business ethics also could change surroundings companies are acting in. Companies show through independent self-obligations that state-introduced regulation is not necessary. And this could be seen as a true entrepreneurial behaviour in terms of freedom of choice. As a further reason for ethical behaviour in business it should not be forgotten that in times of changing values people worldwide might need orientation in their lives as a guideline. Generally religions are no longer seen as the one and only truth. And education while childhood changed dramatically to a higher degree of freedom. Sense and value switching are meant to be mediated by school and state. Unfortunately they sometimes fail as we can often read in newspapers in the recent high numbers of juvenile delinquency. For this reason, employees spend in average about one third of the day at their workstation, firms might substitute to dedicate general an company-individual values, to gain both employer and employee.

But how could this occur by managers? How could ethical behaviour be introduced into daily business? First of all it should be looked at with healthy human understanding. Standards that are valid for conflict-free living since uncountable years, e.g. the Golden Rule,[3] are also a good compass today. Behaviour, criticised as unethical, is often easy to understand as unintelligent and stupid. Of course there would be someone who is fighting for justice. But legal acting is mostly only the minimum. For a second example [Palazzo, G., 2002]. Percy Barnevik, the former CEO of ABB, a Swiss-Swedish company, gained about CHF 148m when he decided to leave the company. It was some kind of 'Goodbye-

---

[1] Think for 'The Body Shop' as an supplier or for the Dow Jones Sustainability Index as an example for higher share prices.

[2] About 88% of the asked companies said that they firstly try to better their intern control systems to prevent white-collar crime. Source: N.A., Ethik und Unternehmenskultur, in: KPMG – Integrity Service (business studies), n.p. 1999

[3] Tobit 4.15: (In a very general manner) What you hate yourself do not do to others.

present'. Unfortunately in this time because of a serious crises in both ABB's market and the company, the firm had to save money wherever it was possible. Therefore their workforce was reduced dramatically and plants had to be closed. Legally there was nothing wrong with this transaction. Mr. Barnevik earned the money (including a 100% bonus from ABB) for his work. But the public might think that there is no economical reasoning for this payment. On one hand people are losing their jobs, the basis for the life of uncountable families, on the other hand one person gets money maybe without any realistic reason.

To become more practical, individually seen managers could follow the ten practical rules (appendix I) published by The Institute of Business Ethics (ibe) in London. This association is acting on behalf of lots of considerable British companies for integration of ethical behaviour within the regular business life. These rules could be seen as some kind of guideline [Spence, 2000]. Summarized can be said that managers should define and communicate core business values and follow these. Furthermore they are supposed to behave in a correct and fair manner to all customers, employees and competitors. And it should not be forgotten that managers' behaviour is seen as a role model to staff. Employees' welfare and motivation might be very important to the firms' future success.

Once managers have decided to behave ethical it is necessary to implement an ethical guideline for both the management and the employees. Therefore as well a publication of the ibe can be used. It is the twelve-step process for implementing a code of business ethics (appendix II) [Le Jeune/Webley, 1998]. Its main flow is to realize demand for ethical action, to compile and to introduce basic principles and to make sure that there is acceptance and cooperation. And its aim is to provide incentives for employees to behave ethically correct. But what does it say exactly? It is seen to be important that a clear strategy is available for code integration. And also that general management endorses the guideline. Without their power the ideas would not be successful. This includes that all members of the firm are responsible for their actions – and that they are clear of this. And finally in the annual report might be a copy to show all shareholders and a wider public companies position in ethical matter. To make such a code more clearly to all who have to behave after it might be good to provide some examples [Bleicher, 1994].

In the end, ethical behaviour might seen to be necessary because of various reasons. They are both individual and collective as well as reasons based on the company and on the society. And there might be less choice for managers because of increasing influence of business in peoples lives and a declining one of state. To secure qualitative production and permanent sales, it can be assumed that every profit oriented company should also think about ethical behaviour. Social responsibility therefore seems to be a great support to gain success for companies, managers – and society.

As shown in the two examples above, Shell and ABB, Managers not only should take the pure figures into account but also the needs and desires of their stakeholders. They could be faced with a lot of different dilemmas to tackle. But managers might should start think in a more human way than only related to revenue and sales - it might be good for all stakeholders. Also because of a more stable customer relationship. And probably the best guideline for current and future managers should be to follow the Golden rule. It's always better not to behave like someone does not want to be treated himself.

# References:

BLEICHER, K., 1994. *Normatives Management - St. Galler Management Konzept* (Band 5). Frankfurt: Campus

CHAMBERS, G., 1998. *The war on talent.* In: McKinsey Quarterly, issue 03/98

DONALDSON, TH., 2001. *No business as usual.* In: Aventis - Future, issue 01/01

DORFS, J., 2001. *Unternehmen entdecken soziale Verantwortung.* In: Handelsblatt, Nr. 021, 30.01.2001

GOVINDARAJAN, V. and TRIMBLE, C., 2002: *Not all profits are equal.* In: Across the board, issue 09/10 2002

KREIKEBAUM, H., 1996. *Grundlagen der Unternehmensethik.* Stuttgart: Schäffer-Poeschel

KALER, J., 2002. *Morality and strategy in stakeholder identification.* In: Journal of Business Ethics, issue 08/2002

LE JEUNE, M. and WEBLEY, S., 1998. *Company use of business ethics.* London: The Institute of Business Ethics. (Available from URL www.ibe.co.uk)

PALAZZO, B., 2001. *Unternehmensethik als strategischer Erfolgsfaktor.* In: io Management, issue 1/2 2001

PALLAZZO, G., 2002. *Legal heisst nicht legitim.* In: Neue Züricher Zeitung, 05.03.2002

SMALL, M.W., 2002. *Practical problems and moral values: Things we tend to ignore revisited.* In: Journal of Business Ethics, issue 09/2002

SPENCE, L., 2000. *Priorities, practise and ethics in small firms.* London: The Institute of Business Ethics. (Available from URL www.ibe.co.uk)

WELSBY, K., 2002. Mammon rules - ethics man is a market loser. In: business a.m., 04.11.2002

WIELAND, J., 1998. *Unternehmensethik in der Praxis – Impulse aus den USA, Deutschland und der Schweiz.* Bern: Haupt

N.A., 1999. *Ethik und Unternehmenskultur.* KPMG – Integrity Service. Frankfurt: KPMG

<u>Appendix I:</u>

## **Ten practical rules for small & medium size businesses for good business conduct[4]**

- Establish your core business values and stick to them or else your reputation will suffer.

- Welfare and motivation of your staff are critical to your success.

- Remember that the owner-manager's business behaviour will be taken as a role model by staff.

- If you need a partner in the business make sure that they share both your vision and values.

- Work at your relations with customers; they neither start nor stop when the sale is made.

- Don't knock your competitors.

- Stick to your agreed terms of payment.

- Record all financial transactions in your books.

- Find at least one way of supporting the communities in which you operate.

- If you are doubtful about an ethical issue in your business, take advice.

---

[4]L. Spence, Priorities, practise and ethics in small firms, The Institute of Business Ethics, London 2000

## Twelve steps for implementing a code of business ethics[5]

1.  **Integration** - Produce a strategy for integrating the code into the running of the business at the time that it is issued.

2.  **Endorsement** - Make sure that the code is endorsed by the Chairman and CEO.

3.  **Circulation** - Send the code to all employees in a readable and portable form and give to all employees joining the company.

4.  **Breaches** - Include a short section on how an employee can react if he or she is faced with a potential breach of the code or is in doubt about a course of action involving an ethical choice.

5.  **Personal Response** - Give all staff the personal opportunity to respond to the content of the code.

6.  **Affirmation** - Have a procedure for managers and supervisors regularly to state that they and their staff understand and apply the provisions of the code and raise matters not covered by it.

7.  **Regular Review** - Have a procedure for regular review and updating of the code.

8.  **Contracts** - Consider making adherence to the code obligatory by including reference to it in all contracts of employment and linking it with disciplinary procedures.

9.  **Training** - Ask those responsible for company training programmes at all levels to include issues raised by the code in their programmes.

10. **Translation** - See that the code is translated for use in overseas subsidiaries or other places where English is not the principal language.

11. **Distribution** - Make copies of the code available to business partners (suppliers, customers etc.), and expect their compliance.

---

[5] M. Le Jeune, S. Webley, Company use of business ethics, The Institute of Business Ethics, London 1998

12. **Annual Report** - Reproduce or insert a copy of the code in the Annual Report so that shareholders and a wider public know about the company's position on ethical matter.

# Mind map on dealing with ethical dilemmas

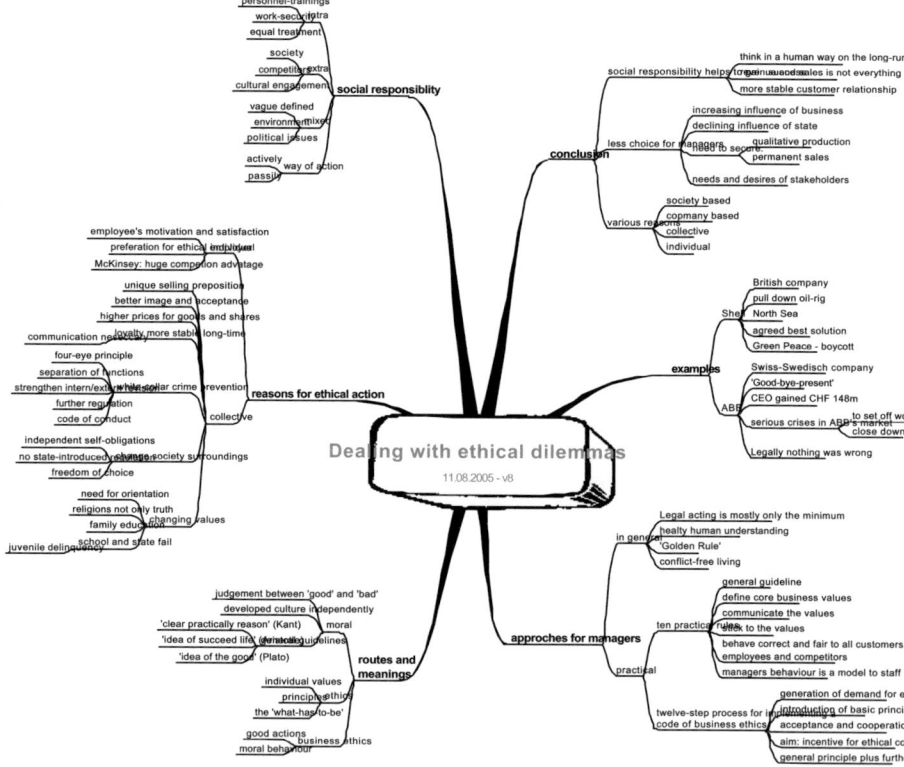